MW00650418

Safe Places for Animals

by Kasey Cooper

Target Skill Draw Conclusions

Scott Foresman
is an imprint of

The land was not safe for big cats like these.

Men hunted them.

But people made safe places for the
cats and other wild life.

Small ducks nested at this safe home.

Big tall cranes rested here too.

Birds are safe here.

Look at this nest in the sand.

Eggs are safe in this home.

It is safe for wild life here.

Look! What have they spotted?

They have a safe place.

They have rocks where they can hide.

People went to the safe places.

They also stopped at this pond.

Fish and frogs are safe in this pond.

People had fun at the safe places.

They looked at ducks and cranes.

They spotted fish and frogs.